10·2·78

HIROSHIMA FLOWS THROUGH US

BROWN MILLER

CHERRY VALLEY EDITIONS

Some of these poems have appeared in the following
periodicals:
*Big Moon, The Coldspring Journal, Contraband,
Corduroy, Grist, New Letters, The New York Quarterly,
Nitty-Gritty, The Ohio Review, San Jose Studies, West
Coast Poetry Review, Xanadu* and *Zahir.*

Library of Congress Cataloging in Publication Data

Miller, Brown.
  HIROSHIMA FLOWS THROUGH US.

1. Hiroshima — Bombardment, 1945 — Poetry. I. Title.
PS3563.I3748H5   811'.5'4   77-22290
ISBN 0-916156-23-0

Typeset by Tin Roof
Printed in the United States of America

2028961

For Sande

Table of Contents

Hiroshima Flows Through Us

Sunset Blossoms Snow

Wings melt back into
a category where eyes
lose their lids and
shine:
>135 days after
Roosevelt's death
analysis and justification
were detonated over
Hiroshima.
>I reach up
and slowly slice off
a chunk of mushroom.

Sitting by myself
in a furrow of night
I eat,
>trusting nothing
to guide me well.

By morning I'm
the snowing of sunset
blossoms.
>By mourning
I'm at home
in any category.

Poem In March

The hospital had a bomb in it.
We went in wearing every dead thing
we'd ever seen or smelled.

She knew our son was dead inside her
even before the tests could
wrap around us and tighten.

The hospital had Hiroshima in it,
coating the walls like fine dust,
covering the floors with shine.

We signed our names with instruments
meant for adding columns of numbers.
The elevators were on film.

I broke my hand against the car window
and drove home unable to see
where I'd been.

I ate food made of bodies,
watched walls sliding through hours,
sliding through my breathing.

I broke my fast against
whatever I had in my hands,
afraid for my mouth to stop.

Two Photographs on Opposite Sides of a Magazine Page

Einstein stares at me from
my window, scares my wife and
daughter at night when they
switch on the light. Day
sends Marilyn through his face.
She flirts from a jumping
position, posed in cement joy.
Einstein's eyes settle in
fatigue, cupped by darkness.
One eye, as big as her breasts,
watches through her belly;
the other looks across the
small of her back. He can't
see Marilyn; she's behind him,
a thickness of paper separating
them enough to prevent bleeding.
His gray skin parts to let her
bright hair, face, and arms
enter the air. Her black
sequin dress cuts diagonally
from above his left eye to his
right jaw. The cheeks of her
buttocks touch and fit the   eks
cheeks of his face. A pen clip
is visible on his sweatshirt
collar; raised veins are visible
on her arms, fists clenching at
caprice. His white hair and
her blonde both serve chaos,
blend. Wrinkles on his
forehead are ropes tied about
her upper torso. Skirt fringe
flings wild to continue his
wild mustache. Her knees
rest in his chin. At night
people of the sidewalk see
them haunting each other.
Marilyn's mouth is open wide
enough to utter Einstein's
century, to swallow his shock.

11

Hiroshima's Nails

I wish I could drop these nails
back where they came from,
all the way back in time
where they held houses together

I want to know how many nails
were melted; the specific number
might let me rest. Or numb me.

I want to compute how many blows
accomplished the inevitable
driving of metal into
departing substance,

though it would be wiser
to count the heartbeats quickened
by each strike of dead precision.

These nails help me come to;
they put me through a hoop
of occult therapy, making me
small enough to fit inside the

sparks flung from impact of hammers
against nails against time,
diminishing me in the
angular cry of friction.

Feed a Fire to Melt Down Grief

the bodies were objects stacks
of logs the rhythm of loading
lulled the able-bodied who
according to strict custom had
to be sure every last one was
cremated by morning
                    it became
automatic we accomplished the
task with little difficulty we
had no emotions it comforted us
to work to exert ourselves to
exhaustion there were so many
of them we soon found the odor
could be ignored
                    the buildings
burned orange but the bodies
blue
        in the past thought to be
the spirits leaving the dead
now known to be the phosphor
in the flesh
                    a replacement who
had just arrived in the area
fell down on the ground when
he saw the flames and was
unable to move.

Fire Says Enough

At the bank I seek counsel from the chained
pens. I'm here to withdraw comfort. After
a lesson as long as my father's car,
I can see the tellers aren't going to tell.

The open vault is full of women with
nothing on but Hitler's mustache. They do
vaudeville routines; they remove spleens from the
public. In the center of the manager's
desk a ram burns for the gods in the wires.

I wake: the burning is my son in the
hospital incinerator. His small smoke
escapes through steel vents. My part is to
make love between this fire and Hiroshima.

No funeral. Fire says enough. The bank
eclipses my eyes, takes away my legs.
The key punch operator sags. I prop her.
Desire hugs me and I collapse inside.

Ocean waves walk me up gravity's crutch.
I work to take myself literally.
I don't budge. The apocalypse lung breathes
for me; neverthefuckingless, our son,
our fetus son....
We were afraid to look at his body.

Poem to Begin April

Hiroshima is in front of me
in the middle of
a shopping center
a suburban ritual
                    Hiroshima
sits in a camera's aim
in a gingerbread house made
of cardboard
                    Easter is coming
but Hiroshima is dressed as
Santa Claus
                    My son's remains
not yet cremated
are displayed in every
store window
                    When I try
to look at them
they move out of my line
of vision
                    move into a blur
His remains
a burlap bag spotted
with tar stains
are alive in my arms
                    I hand him
to Hiroshima who
asks him questions
I listen to everything
remember a name for darkness

The stores close
                    Language harms
without making contact
I am the harm it does

Hiroshima is behind me
kissing my son

Centering Durability Without a Center

Two days of doctors and technicians
took our dead son from her body.
Leaves were finding the ground.

Dead a secret cut of time, he left
us with our words sprawling on the
horizon. They form a circus troupe.
They cross solid rock, oceans of it.
They flow from shadow into shadow.

My edges turn to hard neon,
the only illumination I'll get.
The best or worst. My own.

I lift our son above me, something
dripping on me from his collapsed
head, dripping in my eyes. I lift
him above me to measure him against
Hiroshima, hoping he'll disappear,
wanting him to be swallowed, safe.
But Hiroshima is the one I can't
see, blocked out as neatly as
a single finger covers the sun.

Gound has absorbed the leaves.
Silent, the circus troupe circles.
Our son doesn't wave
or move
except in flame.
We smile deep to breathe him in.

The Code Name

I use Hiroshima to measure.
It's my ruler.
How many inches of pain can I muster today?
I complain of dizziness & loose stools.
Not too convincing.
My wife tells me to stop acting like a baby.
I wish I had a military training film of
the inside of my head.
It would explain the bomb by comparing it to
the sun moved close to the earth for
a few seconds of god-heat.
Kept at enough distance, the sun is our father.
The code name for the bomb was Little Boy.
Come blow your horn.
On the ceiling of the bedroom is a pageant:
Virginia and Vietnam are married.
Their maps fit together nicely, obscenely.
Their histories are sex, one penetrating
the other, exchanging diseases.
Soon a child is born.
Out slides Hiroshima, sly rebirth.
The bomb is its navel.
A twisting umbilical cord drags the mushroom,
a placenta that fills the sky.

Disappearing Infant

I walk miles to dilute the military
training film that shows atomic
explosions from the air and from
the inside, test buildings shredding,
dummies spiraling apart, the whole
desert lowered six feet:

> the narrator's commercial-bred
> voice supplies facts to
> shield us, leaves out details
> like the pilot looking down
> at Hiroshima, entering nothing
> in his log except My God
> and later going blank, going
> mad, electing suicide.

The mushroom took days
to disappear in
the ambivalent currents
changing air to nausea.

> Just before its shape is lost
> my father in Virginia, the
> other side of the world, records
> three more lies in his journal,
> kisses my mother without
> noticing, turns off the light.

I cry in my crib.
(I'm taking years
to disappear.)

When My Father

When my father told me the facts
of life (which he never did) he
left out two: homosexuality and
Hiroshima. If he had tried to
include them (he swears he did)
he would have switched them on
the end of his tongue, their
values disguised as his smile.
He would have put them on top
of each other, pounded them flat,
pounded them flush, then entered
something irrevelant in his
journal, then entered my mother,
shutting me out.
                        As I hunch over
in the hall against their door,
I tell myself Hiroshima never
existed before the explosion,
doesn't exist after it.
I whisper, Hiroshima is the
explosion itself.
                        Twelve years
ago I named my daughter Virginia
when I had no interest in Hiroshima
and thought homosexuality was a bomb.

Sport of Kings

Wind and spirit are the same sound
in Hebrew: the horses are off again.
My kingdom for a horse
to win, place, or show me why
these royal betters lay down
their two dollars as though
laying down their lives for a cause.

My father owns one of those horses
running today; he calls her
Touchdown Miss. A small brown town
in Mississippi? A touchdown
that wasn't made? Touchdown Miss
runs, reminding me of my gone
mother, chasing a dim sun sinking.

The betters go ahead and bet.
They get whatever they get.
Like me she's trying to touch
down. As if racing a sleek death,
she foams, gleams. She was named
for the wrong game: the finish
line is never the goal line,
but our speed stays steady.

The hundreds of thousands of betters
go home; bad weather remains.
Just as I'm about to give it up,
my eyes show me what I missed before.
Look at her! My father's horse!
Animal totem, potent garment.
She explodes down the home stretch
though the sun is perfectly dark.

Clocked by everything I've done,
I know my birth face to face
and feel the reason I'm standing here.
When the touchdown, the real one,
is finally made, and all the horses
lose in empty breath and new rain,
none of us will be afraid.

Our Glands and Talents

Everything I say about Hiroshima belongs
to some other meaning, should blister
from some other awareness.
                              People ask me
(as if they feel) why write about that?
It happened thirty summers ago — why think
about it now?
                I can't tell them Hiroshima
has penetrated everything, is flowing
through us, flies in the sky of our lungs:
I see it, the finest dust in our clothes,
in our hair underwear armpits nostrils,
in our car engines and pocket calculators
and the loges of our theaters, coating
the screens of our televisions,
permeating our softest facial
and toilet tissues, our bones
and connective tissues, our stand-up
comedians, advertisements, political
slogans, our prayers and economy —
invisible — invisible — but I can't
stop seeing it unless I escape
by forgetting, by masturbating.

When these methods fail I use poems
for fallout shelters where I knit
parallels: for example, the H
looks like heroin. So does its
effect — addictive — pervasive.
It greets our glands and talents
with disguised damage and a hot gnaw.

None of this is worthy of itself.
It and I belong a long way off,
in Tibet maybe. In a dim cave.
Or in the belly of a universe
where nothing counts. Or in
a zoo below zero
where feeding is unknown.

August 6, 1975

Hiroshima morning
    exactly
thirty nuclear
    years later

    breakfast
interrupted 200,000
    times
the bomb broke bodies
    like bread

    my son
in a highchair
    softening
in fog: anniversary of
    annihilation

eating orange sections
    eating
segments of Hiroshima

and eaten each minute
    by sixty seconds

Hiroshima Kisses Our Eyes

It hasn't been thirty years
since the bomb put
Hiroshima to bed, tucking
bodies beneath warm smoke.
It hasn't been thirty seconds.

Hiroshima kisses our eyes
wherever, whenever we are
though we think we're snugly
insulated in prefab Now
or reinforced auto chrome Now
or joint high squirming Now.

Hiroshima sips us
through veins of wind.
Hiroshima is a mouth in the sky
sucking us up like soft
drinks.

Morning Routine

Hiroshima waits masked
behind my mirror.

When time is perfect and still
Hiroshima reaches out
and shaves my face,

mistakes each hair
for passion.

Hiroshima holds my penis
while I try to pee,
zips my pants like a dream.

The mirror cracks just enough
to let blood-sweet smoke

slip into air.
I leave for work.
Hiroshima rides the bus with me,

sitting on my lap
like a retarded child.

Circulation of the World's Liquid Assets

I was eating Hiroshima
long before I could taste secret
sweet particles. I am drinking
thin wine of amazing grace.

Everyone worldwide joins me
in an invisible supper
served by the rain. Our mouths bled, bleed,
our tongues limping on languages.

Staid nostrils feed Hiroshima
to continents of lungs, like kilns.
Physical bits of memory
seep through pores from the atmosphere.

A child's heart enters my muscle.
An old man's testicles help my
eyes open and shut and water.
Breasts of pregnancy pass through me.

I have put hours of myself,
fatigued assembly line hours,
into cans of California
peaches. They are deftly sealed,

labeled, boxed, sent across water
in nuclear driven bellies.
Hiroshima eats my thick syrup.
Hiroshima nightmares me home.

You Told Me

I.
Mr. Exner stares through cement air
a ritual as white as my uniform
the slick hospital walls mold me
I don't know his family but
he's more than molecules to be tended
I'm coaxed deeper into his closing
canyon decay   I look for whatever
pieces the cancer hasn't yet taken

he catches me acting out a purpose
he no longer has

I keep his bedpan emptied so he goes on
functioning

he shows me awkward beauty then curses it
mute   hovering above his own torso
in fixed space   I finally smell
the grace of his crooked struggling
closer than my own sweat and dead cells

a valve opens   and a trickle of Hiroshima
                                comes in on us

II.
Mr. Exner
you taught me to discuss Hiroshima the way
most people butter toast   you said
mushroom could be noun or verb
and that McLuhan calls it history's
exclamation point but that it works
more like a question mark
                        if I could
get you into these words (the way I got you
into your pajamas) I might get away
(leave you as a gift   tie Hiroshima
around you in a pretty bow) I might stop
yelling Christ! down my cylinder spine

I don't know if you died or not
I never wrote to find out
I never figured out how to care for real
do you still breathe in there somewhere
pressing waiting breath against waiting
breath? I want to write you silent
with these lines as a gag
closing you in wool laughter

your name keeps coming out of my page
I'm Miss Lonelyhearts bringing his knife
down hard on the lamb's neck but
sacrificing only my poise
sawing the blade against fleece that
gathers dirt to wet blood like magic
and to finish my waking I grab a rock
to crush the lamb's skull   this isn't
for you   this isn't   you had too much
clowning violence crouched mad
on your stainless steel adjustable bed

III.
you told me
Hiroshima was a city in Virginia
I thought you were delirious or
talking through the drugs
until I saw Hiroshima stradle you
hang the stench-breasts down on you
your delicate vampire princess
smiling   giggling   coming
smashing the window with her odor
collapsing into your skeleton

IV.
my first day as an orderly I answered
the light over your door   you wanted me
to get your pajamas on you   it took
twenty minutes of desperate wincing
and anger   and then I discovered
they were on backwards   the whole
pantomime had to be performed again

months later I reminded you of that first
day and it made you smile   almost laugh

we had the ritual perfected   I knew
how to avoid the rubber bag like tense hell
the little pouch on your side where
the excrement collected for emptying

your pajamas meant everything to you
and the bulky white socks seemed to
cushion against pain   you demanded
their presence   they became mysticism

you told me the world was a lovely fat cancer
with Hiroshima the spectacular tumor

V.
how could I be the last thing
you felt like seeing?
you named me Good-bye

I wrapped my voice in shadow
thickened it beyond recognition
I had to forbid our
secrets to kiss

now I try to see you rise
out of the medicines they walled you in

I'm at the edge
of stiff sheets
watching you
clean the opening
in your flesh
a Jesus whose side
bleeds shit
the fragrance of
Hiroshima

I put my hand to my face and you ask
if the smell bothers me

28

you're worrying about my comfort
while torture runs you
through maze after maze

you host your own devouring

the wound in your side glows
agape
and strains to see
the ocean world I map in air

For a Man Who Became Cancer

Our love
is a stack of rewritten
pages, source material
for a furnace.
These images are
crutches walking by
themselves until the
crippled owner claims
them. Our love
is a pile of rags,
each a different
color, waiting
to be sewn into a fool's
costume. I crawl
out of my waste basket.
You told me the money
under the water glass was
mine. Hypnosis hugged
your words, wrapped
my head.
I wanted you to think
I was awake
and could hear
your fist opening,
closing.
The adjustable
steel bed was the only
death I could make sense of.
Our love
had to have lies
at its source.

You and I Are Vanishing

Hiroshima has overflowed its banks
and come down over us

The silt moves softly into us
replaces our bone sorrow with

rushing cold green
and gathered seasons

washing us washing
us washing us

all the way to the
ocean inside us

so we are woven
with the shape of returning.

Secrets

Candles in the long hall of trees
wish their light good-bye.

The air lets the vision hover there
until everything touches silence.

A child lies warm and naked in
feather grass under slightly

broken flowers. The child's
petal throat moves a song

into smooth birth. The song has
no melody or rhythm or intention

of pleasing. None of us knows
how we know it's a song,

but we are as sure of it
as of our steady breathing.

To wrinkled skin the song
is distant sky remembering comets.

Water Play

Near his eighteenth
month, standing on
a chair at the kitchen
sink, my son concentrates
on water, letting it
meditate through his
fingers. A new

intensity comes to him,
miracle of transparent
movement, a shaping
beyond shape. He
controls a cycle
of rebirths in pans
and cups and spoons,
feels himself freed
and flowing untouched
by rigid world.

An initiation of supple
quiet draws into us,
smooth, receptive.
The clear, clarifying
mandala of water
connects origin with end.
The soaking continues
until he reaches for me
and I hug wet joy.

Mirror

Wrinkled woman, blind, reined
to a mangy dog: everything she passes
goes blind, each rail, trash can,
pulse. Her blank glasses
seal in the place I'm curious about.
I watch people help her.
She's willing to touch
any phantom arm.
I don't want this to be my turn
but it is. She fumbles for direction.
She knows I'm here in my breathing.
I stutter an offer.
Not loud enough, but she hears.
Her thin hand ridged with veins,
blue stems, closes on my
sleeve; bones shrink in me.
Lungs sting. My jealousy wrecks
against her voice.
Her words, flowing with night,
hammer me awake.

Ceremonies

I change my name to Hiroshima

I wear Hiroshima around my neck until
the stench teaches me about time

I walk with head down through town
with Hiroshima sewn to my coat
while people point and whisper

In the forest I open my shirt to
show my lover an H burnt on my chest

In the stocks all night I
bow to a painful erection

I sow Hiroshima's teeth in asphalt
and cringe at the sudden crop
an alphabet of armed devices
I smell language on the altar

On the banks of the Hiroshima
I stand waiting to wade in
for baptism and an ear infection

I hang Hiroshma for murder

I hang Hiroshima out the window
of a speeding car   my bare moon
The windshields behind me
bloom with wet ashes

The Right to Squirm

The bomber's code name was Bo-Peep.
Little Bo-Peep has lost her sheep
and can't tell where to find them.
I go to Sherlock Holmes for comfort,
but near morning I've been convicted
in Hiroshima's courtroom of contortion.
Copies of Holmes, some in English,
most in Japanese, copies of Mother
Goose, maps of Virginia, all went up
in micro-bits, blasted at the heavens
to billow breastlike above the fires.

I saw Hiroshima in half on stage each
night and rave inside with peace.
Just as we dismount our dreams, I tell
Bo-Peep not to lose sleep over lost
sheep, not to worry about their tails.
Holmes shares his cocaine with Bo-Peep.

Hiroshima's mama was Pearl Harbor.
Later they flew ganders together
above a Vietnam casino owned by
Mother Goose, sucking thumb after
thumb for brave boys, the way I suck
Hiroshima's stones to create saliva,
sucking a tit which is a cock, a snake.
I study Hiroshima's voice and mannerisms,
another impression for my Vegas act.
Gambling shrinks my head to size of
reason, coaxes me to relax with
spells cast by the nostalgia of those
first, dirty A bombs, black and white
Saturday afternoon movies. Hiroshima:
a refrain touching each cell indelibly.

I Read My Father's
Virginia Journal

while his money moves back and forth through me
like thread following a needle   my anger
tips itself upside-down in a blind spot where
I can see his prejudices get into the saddle
on my back   cinched solid   the spurs dig

my fever registers on no thermometer
my mother's cerebral blood vessel ruptures
into paralysis   into monologue   ten days
later into death during a summer that made me
seven   I keep fighting for fantasies to keep
her supple   edible   sexual
    she is multiple faces made of wind

Mr. Exner goes on dying of cancer when I'm
seventeen in New Jersey   playing
the orderly and the whore   washed by
hospital air-conditioning relentlessly
he maintains a spare consciousness: mine

I research the role of withered rock gardens
and how witchcraft brewed in Hiroshima's caldron
beginning with the Reverend Mr. Tanimoto on TV
in 1974 saying "if Japan had had the bomb
we would have used it on you   the guilt
is your problem"
    but his eyes do not translate

my son dies before he can push into his birth
Sherlock Holmes goes home   goes dumb
Mother Goose runs out of advice for Bo-Peep
I keep track of pointless transactions like
pneumonia   I fart in case I have to find
my way out of here   it should be pointed out
that television is pointillism and Hiroshima
is a dissolution into scattering omnipresent
points (so I keep score until I go limp)

Critical Mass, Without Priest

when I was tending
Mr. Exner's bouquet of cancer
talking to his dying
watering it daily   nightly

he turned to me from the
concentration camp once his body
and explained that the Nazis
had an enormous hungry number
of small ovens

whereas in the name of
freedom & democracy
on a mass scale we
found it more suited to
our needs to use a few fast
vast ovens like
  Dresden
      Nagasaki
        Hiroshima

Mr. Exner smiled enough to
scare me saneless
and summed up our lucid
solution: we brought
the mountain to Mohammed

Mechanisms

I read Lifton to get bombed:
"the unconscious process here
is that of closing oneself off
from death   the controlling
inner idea or fantasy is 'if
I feel nothing then death
is not taking place'   psychic
closing off is thus related
to the defense mechanisms of
denial and isolation as well as
to the behavioral state of
apathy"* mechanisms   mechanisms
mechanisms   Mr. Exner's cancer
walled off where he can't touch
me   walled in with the three
corpses I lugged into refrigerated
formaldehyde drawers after
tying baggage tags on their
toes   mechanisms   mechanisms
like Lifton's prose style wedged
firmly between each loosening
nerve while murders on TV
score hit after hit walled off
where sensibility can't be
felt or felt up
or pinched or sucked off
or pinned to a heart

*From "History and Human Survival" by Robert Jay Lifton.
Copyright 1971 by Robert Jay Lifton. Reprinted by permission.

Hiroshima, Virginia, Wet Dream

Covered with the tar and feathers
of a pimp's libido, I stare at them.
I want Virginia to touch Hiroshima,
inhale its chill breath like time,
bodies in a vaporized orgy sucked
into the pure stalk of hot tornado.

Virginia, fathering my authority
repeatedly, anchors my birth, severe
component of whatever blood is left.
The myths go on wobbling,
delapidated, held up only
by a brittle scaffold: duty.

    I'm sucking my thumb
    when the bomb
    drops. My diapers
    change automatically
    at the pinch of
    numb desire.

I stare backwards: Hiroshima
evaporates me, nullifies hungers.
I squint its round cloud into
a mirage of breast flesh for my lips.
The sucking takes me to puberty.

Virginity, or its political mask,
wants me to push Virginia against
Hiroshima. With dry mouth I watch
the dense tower of nudes. The lethal
mushroom moves its head up inside,
pushes rich miscegination, mixing.

The shadow of smoke mounts white fire,
fathers a mother whose tears can kill.

Third Elbow

the mushroom above
the wrinkling smoothing wrinkling
city
is a doorknob
inside is the Civil War
and water rushing over John Turner's head
his skull opened under a car's tire
swimming at Clear Creek the kids wanted
to move the car closer so they could hear
the radio and dance to it

a doorknob
inside is my mother's paralysis
ambassador of brain hemorrhage
in whose still rape she lay motionless for
ten days before the coma would
let her relax into earth

a doorknob
inside is Virginia playing her flute
getting her braces tightened
doing homework and waiting for Halloween
Christmas Easter and everything chocolate
and farther inside is Virginia the state
its trees and grass the color and consistency
of a gas flame   the Blue Ridge Mountains
humming slow-motion rage to
bolster the people's constipated conventions

the doorknob cloud blooms
        it is my cerebrum
        surpassing the force
        of a drum's polemic
        heard from the inside

Oven Fresh

I make Mr. Tanimoto sit
on the porch of his plantation home
and sip mint juleps through
my veins
                   I have Dr. Sasaki draw his
Confederate sword to examine it
for rust stains or Yankee blood while
considering self-castration in front of
the slaves
              I let Mrs. Nakamura
take a nap to the music of gray
uniforms while fields burn
toward her bed
                  it's a dream I
haven't had yet   but it's had me

from between its skinny legs
I flopped wet   blue
                   I'm unable
to stop taking root wherever
I light
        I can't stabilize my eyes
nor assign myself a normal perspective

I will be the doorknob on the
bomb's oven door
                pulled in
unconscious directions
                   fatigue (like
plush fungus)
           will cushion
     the bump
of insight

Hiroshima Postcard

I write from Hiroshima, Virginia
a little place at the base
of my cranial mountains

a field floods
floats Mr. Exner toward me
tangled in the debris of tumors

and floats toward me my
son's afterbirth (a silence
makes it all invisible)

in a laboratory like sky
or a sky that never varies
I experiment on Hiroshima's nails

I want to taste how they
melted in the slightest
suggestion of time-lapse

then hardened in the image of
new lettuce leaves like the ones
I cultivated from city soil

this nail is an old woman's cane
this one a zen monk's staff going
through the palm of my mind

Virginia Winter

I wait for Hiroshima's
cherry tree cloud
to nurse me: it doesn't

but I'm hung up
in the branches
waiting in gray tangling
tangled gray waiting
for its skirt to come clean
and spread me in its wake

Easter is my mask

I've gone down thirty
years wearing my mother's
brain for a headband
pretending torn tissues
will mend before I
feel them tear again

I choose the loveliest
sights to hide myself

I want to be near mountains
when unwinding coils
bloom open and squirm
on each of my nerve limbs

these lines are woods
draped with a
deadly healing thickness
of snow knowledge

44

Hiroshima's Part in the Civil War

The Old South rises
in Hiroshima's steaming miracle,
spreads black sky.
Blurring through me, the clouds
bow politely, beautifully
composed in hundred mile per hour
winds. At Appomattox
Grant and Lee hold Hiroshima
between their teeth,
toss it back and forth, scrub it
between words and belches.
Lee's sword is mistaken for radiation
mingled with surrender.
Grant's decorations look like
shelter or stupor.
Grant is unwrapping a city's fire
from his dollars.
Lee uniforms himself in
a chivalry of flesh tapestries
so torn
they reveal everything.
Grant is Lee,
rolling in anonymous stench,
swollen bellies of smoke
covering Japan and collapsed horses.
Pomp crackles, fits
down inside corpse after corpse.
Their beards are pubic hair.
This sleep of ours
is the lead casing on polished bombs.

Obese Omen

Hiroshima breaks me into insects, dissolves me
each time I blink. Hiroshima wipes my ass
to get rid of images that stink up my voice.

How many times is Hiroshima's name going to
come out of my typewriter like a terrible tongue?

I swallow frying fat: it's Hiroshima
burning a column of genocide all the way
to my anus. Scalded fish rise in my mirror.

Skin gone but still walking, people make
their way from the center where the city was.
They move through a peculiar haze
gauzed over ground.
Corpses surround the walkers,
accuse and convict them of survival,
lock them up for life.
Collapsed houses moan from crushed innards.

For water I drink Virginia, my birth.
Orgasms don't fit me anymore; they've
outgrown me. I want to deny this omen.
I want to kill it by chanting Oven Oven Oven.

But something ripples my flesh, reminds me
I'm made of nothing but omens.
Omens in open bloom.
My name turns to compost before I can say it.
Good rains fall in me.

Hiroshima nods as we pass on the street.

Safe in the Owl's Talons

I am in a hallway of rubber/coal/uranium.
The leading citizens sneeze
and are led off.
Rats have gotten into the sky
and run like the mad among stars.

Pneumonia weeds flank me.
Entrails of vultures are found cuddled
in the bellies of senators.
Human sighs fit perfectly
in electric generators.

My veins appear off and on
in gnarled wood.
Black helicopter ghosts beat
air down on me. Ambulances loaded
with image defects stop my
thoughts like needles of morphine.

I smell the ocean, lean down
and touch the sand of my own flesh.

When I Was an Orderly

I needed rituals.
Everything kept away
from me
and I didn't know it.
Anything could have been
my ritual: any
enema or backrub or
pulse. My hunger
was a twisting core
that came out when
I thought about
crying. She asked me
if I'd ever sat
down and just cried,
cried long and
completely.
I had to say no.
She was one of
the last rooms
at the end of
the cancer hall.
Both breasts.
What was her name?

She Was Sixteen When I Was Born

my sister   a brain tumor at age 49   with a
string of small tumors along her spine
bitter little mushroom buttons
sedentary bullets
for 25 years she worried that she would die
of a brain hemorrhage the way Mother had
the head always the head
her last eleven years she fought to rise in
the credit department of a trucking firm
pushing to make as much money as a man
when they heard she had cancer they let her
go as quickly & politely as possible
when it was certain she would be dead in a
matter of months I took a jet to see her
able to afford a three-day weekend
the jet comforted me in its sound & alcohol
cortisone met me at the airport   stood there
wearing a distortion of my sister held up by
her family   she was surreal   she was
nauseating as hope   had a parody of a face
horrible chipmunk with a hump on her back
the way cortisone demanded and bald from
the cobalt   her mock pregnant belly
cortisone's doing   made her talk of her
children's births   she joked everything in
my face   freed from caring about overeating
scrambling her family like eggs   and when
her son asked her not to eat all the
peanut butter
she told him to drop dead

after dinner at a fine restaurant she stepped
in a shallow hole in the parking lot and
fell down in front of our father
who couldn't catch her

I'd been home for two months when they
stopped the cortisone and she went into
a coma, death's waiting room.

Hiroshima's Dishwashing Detergent

My dead sister's dishwasher
asks me to feed it full
of Hiroshima's dust

but I'm in prison and can't help.

The tumor in my sister's
head
asks me for Hiroshima's address
and Marilyn Monroe's sequins
and Einstein's mustache clippings
and a ritual good for one time only
and a candle that answers like birth
and a death that goes down like candles.

Suddenly our picture takes us,
a red odor
coming in the frontdoor
to sit with us
as polite as an insurance man.

Hiroshima's camera
asks my dead sister to load it
full of clean new space

but she's visiting my prison
and carrying her life's supply
of dishwashing detergent and
determined to save herself for
the man in the moon.

Penis Corpse

Penis gets up from grave,
puts on costume balls like
jewelry, manages wings and goes
for the sky's throat, draws
red rain from thin blue skin.
Penis, where did you
come from? Why
do you fly fast and south
through whatever you're given?
Penis never answers, wants
secrets for feathers.
Penis jacks off too near
the sun, falls, drips wax.
On railroad tracks Penis
is a locomotive, pulls
hissing balls on basic black
like big pearls, pulls
empty boxcars strung
on a rattling spine, sprays
thick sperm smoke at the clouds.
Penis goes a hundred
down the Amtrack nerve,
vanishes in a tunnel
to emerge through televised
meditation. Penis does a
Cagney Yankee Doodle Dandy
and returns to corpse.
Penis has been sniffing
the Japanese capital gain,
nostalgic for old romance.
What a way to get laid.

Its Hour Come Round at Last

From ground that once
grew Hiroshima grow
plants manufacturing
Mazdas, Dodge Colts,

restaurants welcoming
Diner's Club, Mastercharge,
chains of Mr. Doughnut
revolving day and night.
Nothing was rebuilt.

It all had to be new
to cover the smudge.
In these clean buildings
time-released capsules
are swallowed reverently.

The new money serves
as scar tissue so no one
recalls the numb splendor.
The new money prays.

Hiroshima hides in its
business address, summons
executives who court
clients with dinners and
gambling and massage.

Survivors do not survive.
August 6, 1945: the dawn
came as a bomb, born
inconveniently. There
was no room at the inn.

Hiroshima is a Member of My Family

waits politely to use the bathroom
refuses to help set the table or
wash the dishes or do the laundry
wants the television on all night
asks for everything advertised
expects to be treated like a guest
expects to float through walls
and win arguments with the nails
and evade the issue of the pipes
and race the wiring to the switches
expects great things from me
from my daughter and son
expects my wife to understand
a death with a life of its own
but politeness slips everything
past us like a clawless cat
while clothes need ironing
and words clog the drains
and certain hinges
cry louder than August sun

Is That Hiroshima or My Mother?

She gets up to explain how she died,
demonstrating how lively she can

seem. She adjusts her skin,
reaches out for an adjoining

desperation, then covers my head
with catlike licking, her tongue

missing nothing except the
sad scab where I failed to perform

the way one wife demanded and
another wife needed. Her saliva

replies to my whines, adheres
to my habit of sneaking pity out.

I could use at least two heads
and all the hearts my arms could

hold. Mother convincingly
impersonates Hiroshima, or the

reverse. She fastens night
to her blouse, swings moss over

her shoulders, and stands there
at my door, counting each one

of my fears until she can remember
the name she left me in to die.

Table Manners Gained at a Sizzling Cost

My father gets up from his
buttlike chair
and calls Hiroshima the horse
to come produce my sister
from its throat.
She slides out on a ribbon
of slime. Sad blizzards
park in my ears, wait to be
towed. My obligations
are thrown into gas chambers
like rapists or kidnappers.
I don't know who's behind this.

Gathering herself about her
spine, my sister comtemplates
my boils, then begins
pricking them open.
The 6 O'Clock News reaches
my quick, stretches me out
over an anvil; the 11 O'Clock
News is the hammer that
shapes me to fit
Hiroshima's hooves.
I release my fumes
to crawl and creep up toward
sacred light fixtures.
Hiroshima hits a home
run, snuffs out
vowels.

Predator

Hiroshima perches in a tower
watches me drink tea

The spell is in the tea
and in the drinking of the tea
a ritual designed by time
to tighten its fluid skin

My movements glow through curtains
weave in and out of my arms

Hiroshima ruffles its feathers
watches me pour tea
down the drain

I sit here in Japan
with Japan in my hands
folding itself
in my suspended hands

I go liquid in a coward's fever
inventing the worst diseases for my head

Drinking tea should be my lens through which
I could judge my past judgements and
 detach my life to see where I should see

Hiroshima sharpens a claw
watches me write about drinking tea

I drank a false lead
the clue was in the preparing and serving
and posture

the lens eludes the eye
folds into the tea
a sea without waves
my throat tears

Shimmering Membrane Gloves You

Hiroshima, have I taken you for granted?
Should you divorce me because I enjoy
the guilt of sleeping with other, younger
atrocities? Hiroshima, you became a whore
to become a virgin. You took my hand and
led me to a bed in the sky. Why must we
do this to each other? The bed is plush
with all your famous bodies strewn as far
and wide as the future, rich naked stew.
Each skin was neatly removed and hidden.
Hiroshima, why do I have to dress you up
again and again in word after word? I'm
tired. Aren't your pale gown of vapor
and your ash blond hair decent enough?
Hiroshima, you are a virus entering me
through an umbilical thirty years long
and getting longer. Your explosion
enters the worming word of your name
into the hearts of my poems. I have no
privacy; all my images are wire-tapped.
I can't stop calling you names, sticking
my tongue out at you, giving you the finger.
Hiroshima, massage my back & legs & prick.
You make me sick, yet I long for a touch.
Hiroshima, I've gradually become your
mother. How is the womb-wandering today?
Can you feel my veins bloom all around you
and my circulation keeping you whole?
Hiroshima, you are getting terribly old.
You age a hundred years for every one of
mine; soon no one will care about you.
You'll be stranded in a nursing home,
dark. With pee stains on your sheets,
you'll mumble. They'll tie you down, let
lice live in your underwear forever.

Virginia Takes Hiroshima
by the Hand

and they attend the death
of Malcolm X.
They are present at his burial,
stung by black, stretched
easy. Virginia takes Hiroshima by
the handful.
They are future at the birth
of Angela Davis, becoming the past
at her last will. In between
there's time
for Malcolm to put his mind against her stomach
and, though broken,
sing.
        Virginia takes Hiroshima by
surprise. They stand
outside the fence while
George Jackson goes down; they
are sweating on flowers.
Hiroshima and Virginia
are absent at their own death,
vacationing in some
Caribbean uterus,
uneasy.

Learning Music

Virginia hears Hiroshima's bomb
crying
    She picks it up
    cuddles and rocks it
    the way she would a lover's
    severed arm

She feeds the bomb from her body
then puts it across her knee
and burps it

Across my knee is a stringed
instrument that I've never
seen before   but I'm
able to play it
to weave whatever I feel
without looking at my
fingers or anyone's pain

Virginia listens
understands or doesn't
bathes the bomb and diapers it

I focus the song
on the nape of her neck
silk comfort
    "know when you see him
    nothing can free him"

Virginia lets the bomb take
everything she has

Her promises are lakes
without surface or bottom
(she goes gently azure
having always wanted
a doom of her own)

Eternal Apprenticeship

Virginia nurses Hiroshima.
They switch identities
and sprout ambiguities like antlers.
Hiroshima nurses Virginia.
One of them is red-nosed rain;
the other wears a white beard
hiding classified information
on snowflakes of human skin.

Children have been pressed
against blue-gray, flattened
into patterns. When I look up
from my birth, the mushrooming flame
is nipple is sucking is burp is sleep.
Garbagemen wield early morning
and morning welds me awake.

Virginia is three syllables;
Hiroshima is four: the second
of each is stressed, the
signature of a heartbeat.
Hiroshima, Virginia: enough
to make the middle line of
a haiku I'm waiting to write,
wanting to make it with sounds
beyond words, to make room for
the mush we keep making of life.

My part is to stay on the make
for metaphor until war earns
its own living, and the body is
christened as well as the head,
and I make off with the reason
we make our lies come true
and find out how to make love
as though nobody's life depended
on somebody's dying.

Invisible Deliverance

dance with honest pretense
and dump pretended honesty

each image my benefactor
and my jailer

it doesn't matter
what matters is my desire

to find and keep one place
in this gradual avalanche of

delirium (a burning hospital
will do) where poetry

can't get in to wipe its feet
I want one place where

we can agree to surrender
to what we were

before that Godzilla called
language woke up and put

its tongues through our minds
(we'll chirp like organic wit

carried back to young Virginia
our virgin excuses tangible enough

to bite) as our ribs fade
we rise out of our bonds

quietly on fire:
released.

photo: Joel Deutsch

About The Author

Brown Miller was born in Front Royal, Virginia in 1943, on a battlefield of one war during the waging of another. He grew up in a small town in northern California. He has worked as an embalmer of laboratory animals, a peach cannery warehouseman, a janitor, a hospital orderly, a file clerk and an encyclopedia salesman. Flunked out of U.C. Berkeley as a science major; attended Merritt College in Oakland as an art major; ended up at San Francisco State University as a creative writing student under Mark Linenthal and the late Arthur Foff, both of whom he regarded as mentors. A.B. and M.A. in creative writing from S.F. State. In 1967 he began teaching at City College of San Francisco, where he has designed a course in poetry writing and co-designed one in a mixed media approach to poetry and photography. He has had over 200 poems published in some 40 literary magazines since 1965; has edited an anthology called *Lung Socket* in 1969 (Open Skull Press); has had several chapbooks published, some of which are *Fertilized Brains* (Open Skull), *Autopsies & Family Ghosts* (Runcible Spoon), *Whiskeytown Iron Mountain Triptych* (Molly Moon), *Waters & Shadows* (Twowindows), *The Liquid Child's Sun* (Black Rabbit). He presently reviews poetry books for *Small Press Review* and *Nitty-Gritty*, and is west coast editor for *Northeast Rising Sun*. Work in progress: *Writing Poems from the Inside Out: Craft as Growth of Consciousness.*

$2.50
Cherry Valley Editions
Box 303
Cherry Valley,
New York 13320